1 MONTH OF
FREE
READING

at
www.ForgottenBooks.com

By purchasing this book you are eligible for one month membership to ForgottenBooks.com, giving you unlimited access to our entire collection of over 1,000,000 titles via our web site and mobile apps.

To claim your free month visit:

www.forgottenbooks.com/free291887

ISBN 978-0-484-41262-9
PIBN 10291887

THE MANGER

A MIRACLE PLAY
IN THREE ACTS

BY

CLARKE SMITH

M86911

DEC 27 1913

To
CHARLES N. NELSON, 3D

A limited edition of this book printed by THE JENSON PRESS in Philadelphia, for private distribution.

Act I.   *A Room in the Aunt's House.*

Act II.   *The Cross-Roads.*

Act III.   *The Carter's Home.*

—————

TIME

Christmas Eve.

CHARACTERS

The Woman

The Aunt

The Child

The Voice

The Carter

The Drover

The Shepherd

The Peddler

The Young Man

The Waits

Celestial Voices

The Horse

The Dog

The Fox

The Donkey

The Goat

The Bird

The Pheasant

The Grouse

The Hare

The Rabbit

ACT I

THE MANGER

ACT I

(*The interior of the living-room of* THE AUNT's *house.*

The room is plainly furnished. Over the mantel is a large copy of Rubens' "Descent from the Cross." A fire burns on the hearth. A door in the center of the back opens directly into the yard.

When the curtain rises, THE AUNT *is seated in a rocking-chair in front of the fire.*)

AUNT.—What a fearful night! The wind is piling up the snow and soon will block the roads. God help the travelers abroad this Christmas Eve!

(*A knock is heard.* THE AUNT *beside the fire does not hear it. A second knock, a little less timid than the first. The woman turns her head and listens. A third knock, this time quite audible above the noise of the wind.*)

AUNT (*starting up, then hesitating*).—What is that sound? Maybe some one outside is seeking shelter from the storm.

(*A fourth knock.* THE AUNT *rises and walks toward the door, then hesitates, as if afraid to open.*)

AUNT.—Who can it be? Some stranger, likely, who has wandered from the way. 'Tis Christmas

Eve. The storm grows worse. A dog would perish on a night like this. I'll open and admit whoever is outside.

(THE AUNT *starts to draw the bolt.*)

VOICE (*outside*).—Open, open in the Christ-Child's name.

(THE AUNT *draws the bolt. The door opens slowly and a woman, wet, bedraggled, and covered with snow, staggers in and leans, breathing heavily, against the wall inside the room. The door, through which the falling snow can be distinctly seen, remains open.*)

AUNT.—Come near the fire and warm yourself. Your garments and your feet are soaked. Sit here beside the blaze. I'll fetch you something warm to drink and then a bite to eat.

(THE WOMAN *stands motionless.* THE AUNT *looks at her in astonishment, unable to understand* THE WOMAN'S *failure to accept her invitation. She walks up to her and takes her by the arm.*)

AUNT.—Come.

(THE AUNT *leads her toward the fire. The fire-light shines upon* THE WOMAN'S *face.* THE AUNT *suddenly removes her hand from* THE WOMAN'S *arm and starts as though stung by a poisonous reptile.*)

AUNT (*hoarsely*).—You? You?

THE WOMAN (*faintly*).—Yes, AUNT, 'tis I.

AUNT (*with rising anger*).—How dare you cross the threshold of this house?

WOMAN.—O, AUNT, for *pity's* sake!

AUNT (*pointing to the door*).—Begone!

WOMAN (*raising her hands before her face, as though warding off a blow*).—O, no, no, no! My strength is spent. I have no place to go. For God's sake, give me shelter for to-night!

AUNT (*sternly, pointing to the door*).—Go!

WOMAN (*falling upon her knees*).—For God's sake, let me stay!

AUNT.—Rise from your knees and go!

WOMAN.—My hour has come. My woman's hour.

AUNT (*hoarsely*).—Shameless, begone!

WOMAN.—My frame is racked with pain. My hour has come. O, let me stay!

AUNT (*stamping angrily*).—Begone, I say, begone!

WOMAN.—My child will perish in the snow ere it begins to live. O, let me stay!

AUNT.—'Twere better so; begone!

WOMAN (*stretching her arms toward the picture of the Crucifixion above the mantel*).—Then for the sake of Him on yonder cross, who, too, was born on Christmas Eve, have mercy on the little life beneath my heart and let me stay.

AUNT.—Blasphemous wanton, leave this house! Your presence is pollution.

WOMAN.—O, say not so. I've done no wrong. (*Pointing toward the picture.*) I swear it by yon thorn-crowned head.

Aunt (*wringing her hands in impotent fury*).—O, sacrilege! O, shameless *blas*phemy! How *dare* you take that *sacred* name u*pon* your *sinful lips?* Begone, begone!

Woman (*imploringly*).—O, *do* not turn me out to die! O, let me *stay!*

Aunt.—If *such* as you can die, then die!

Woman.—Have you no heart within your *breast?* I am your *sister's* child.

Aunt.—You are no kin of mine.

Woman.—You, too, have felt beneath your heart a little life, and by this memory, so *sweet* to woman, let me stay *just* for to-night.

Aunt.—I was a wife—

Woman.—And so am I.

Aunt.—Show me your *ring*.

Woman.—I *pawned* it to get here.

Aunt (*laughing mockingly*).—She *pawned* her *wedding*-ring! Ha! ha!

Woman.—It was too far to walk with the *burden* that I bear.

Aunt.—Where is your *document* to *prove* you are a wife?

Woman (*despairingly*).—Alas! dear Aunt, I've lost it, too. I had it here (*pointing to her breast*), *pinned* fast, but it is gone.

Aunt.—No *wedding*-ring—no *document!* (*With intense scorn.*) And yet you call yourself an honest woman? Away! Begone! My *roof* shall never shelter such as you.

WOMAN.—You loved my mother once. For her sake let me stay!

AUNT.—Not for a single hour!

WOMAN.—Then by your mother's anguish when you entered life, her travail and her *pain*—

AUNT (*shaken, but determined*).—Begone at once!

WOMAN.—Think of your hour so long ago, and yet so sweet. Think and be merciful to me!

AUNT.—Once more I tell you, go!

WOMAN (*throwing her arms around the* AUNT's *knees*).—Be merciful! Not for myself, but for the little child to be!

AUNT (*struggling to free herself*).—Unloose your arms! Unloose and go!

(THE AUNT *finally succeeds in freeing herself and moves away from* THE WOMAN. *The latter continues kneeling, with her face buried in her hands. She removes them and stretches her arms toward the picture above the mantel.*)

WOMAN.—O, Thou who camest to earth on Christmas Eve, whose ear is never deaf to pity's cry, in pain and want I turn to Thee. My hour has come, my woman's hour! No home, no shelter from the wintry blast, except beneath this roof, where my unhappy girlhood days were spent. I never knew a father's love. My mother *died* while I was but a child and left me to her elder *sister's* care. She gave me food and clothes, but never love. I grew

21

to womanhood, friendless, alone. And when love came, my frozen heart was melted like the ice in spring, and I began to live. All Nature was transformed beneath love's glow. This house became a palace wherein I dwelt, a princess—a willing slave, who loved her fetters and found bondage sweet. I kept my secret hidden in my heart. It was my first, my only one. I had no friend in whom I could confide. I dared not share my secret with my AUNT, and so I loved, as I had always lived—alone.

(*She remains silent for a moment, gazing intently at the face of the Crucified.* THE AUNT *stands motionless, her features seem turned to stone. After a brief silence,* THE WOMAN *continues.*)

WOMAN.—Nay, I was wrong. There was One Friend, the Friend of all who turn to Him. I turned to Thee as plants turn toward the sun, and there was nothing hid. At length, I told my AUNT and asked her blessing and consent. She drove him from her door and woke me from my dream with threats of curses and of banishment. At length one night, when all things were asleep, I fled, two hours before the dawn, and ere the sun rose o'er the eastern hills we two before God's altar were made one. A year of happiness, and then, before the crowning joy of motherhood, they brought him lifeless to our humble home.

(THE WOMAN, *overcome, buries her face in her hands.* THE AUNT *stands, cold and pitiless, without a trace of sympathy on her countenance.*)

WOMAN.—In my *despair*, I turned once more to beg for shelter at the han*d*s of one who share*d* the same maternal breast with my dea*d* mother. Her heart is har*d*: O, *s*often it! She think*s* me vile: O, *p*rove me *p*ure! She drive*s* me forth: O, bid her let me *s*tay!

(THE WOMAN *gazes imploringly at the Crucified. THE AUNT's countenance reveals the various emotions at war within her. Pity and hatred struggle for the mastery. She hesitates, makes an involuntary movement toward the kneeling woman, and then, as if ashamed of her momentary weakness, assumes her former cold and pitiless expression. She approaches* THE WOMAN *and takes her by the arm.*)

THE AUNT.—Enough! I'll hear no more. The air within thi*s* room is *p*oisoned by your bla*sp*hemy. Begone, at once!

(THE WOMAN *rises from her knees and walks slowly toward the door, casting one last despairing glance at the picture above the mantel. As she reaches the door and sees the falling snow, she recoils with a shudder. The wind sends a flurry of snow into the room.*)

WOMAN.—'Tis death to venture forth.

AUNT.—Begone!

WOMAN (*in desperation, turning with clasped hands to the aunt*).—O, let me stay?

AUNT (*thrusting her through the door*).—Begone!

(THE WOMAN, *with a cry* of *anguish, disappears in the snow and darkness.* THE AUNT *closes the door and bolts it, after which she approaches the fire and stands, facing the flames. She lifts her eyes gradually from the fire and fastens them on the picture. Slowly, but without removing her eyes, she sinks upon her knees. The eyes in the picture grow stern.* THE AUNT, *unable to bear their mute accusation, covers her face with her hands. A trembling seizes her. She rocks to and fro, half moaning, half sobbing. Suddenly she rises and rushes to the door. With feverish haste she draws the bolt and flings the door wide open. The snow enters in big gusts and the wind shrieks fiercely.* THE AUNT, *unmindful* of *the snow and cold, stands in the center* of *the door and calls out into the darkness.*)

AUNT.—Come back! Come back!

(*The wind echoes her words, or seems to do so, mockingly.*)

AUNT (*wildly*).—I was mad! I did not mean it! Come back!

(*The wind shrieks mockingly.*)

AUNT (*sobbing and wringing her hands*).—Alas! she hears me not! God help us both!

(*She returns to the fire, leaving the door wide open. She throws herself on her knees and raises her arms toward the picture. The eyes* of *the Crucified are full* of *mournful reproach.*)

VOICE.—Suffer little children—

AUNT (*sobbing*).—Oh, oh, oh!

24

VOICE.—To come unto me,—

AUNT (*wringing her hands*).—Oh, oh, oh!

VOICE.—For of such is—

AUNT (*moaning convulsively*).—Oh, oh, oh!

VOICE.—Is the Kingdom—

AUNT (*rocking to and fro*).—Oh, oh, oh!

VOICE.—Of Heaven.

AUNT (*tearing at the neck of her dress*).—I am choking! Give me air!

VOICE.—Inasmuch as ye did it not—

AUNT (*gasping*).—I am strangling!

VOICE.—To one of the least of these—

AUNT.—I am *dying*!

VOICE.—Ye did it not—

AUNT.—Have mercy!

VOICE.—To me.

AUNT (*throwing herself prostrate on the floor and bowing her head on her clasped hands*).—Lost! Lost! Lost!

VOICE (*repeating very slowly*).—To me.

AUNT.—O, say not so! Not unto Thee!

VOICE (*sadly*).—To me.

AUNT (*raising her head*).—I will atone.

VOICE.—Too late, too late!

(*The wind dies down. Suddenly a low, wailing sound is heard.* THE AUNT *raises herself to a sitting position and listens. The wailing continues with brief intervals of silence. She covers her ears with her hands to shut out the sound. After a few moments, she rises and staggers toward the open door. She leans against the side of the door, her chin resting on her breast. The wailing becomes more distinct. THE AUNT raises her hands as if trying to ward off the sound.)*

AUNT (*shuddering*).—It is a feeble infant's cry.

VOICE.—Wrapped in swaddling clothes—

AUNT (*listening attentively*).—A little, helpless child—

VOICE.—Lying in a manger—

AUNT.—Dying in the snow!

VOICE.—For unto us a Child is born—

AUNT.—I drove the child away.

VOICE.—Unto us a Child is given—

AUNT.—I spurned the gift.

VOICE.—He shall gather the lambs with his arm—

AUNT.—I mocked its helplessness.

VOICE.—And carry them in His bosom—

AUNT (*overcome by the enormity of her deed*).— I am undone!

(She staggers to the center of the room, raises her white, despairing face toward the Crucified, and extends her arms.)

AUNT (*slowly*).—There came to me, on Christmas Eve, a woman and a child. They came, too, in

Thy Name, but I was blind and could not see. Hungry—I fed them not; thirsty—I gave no drink; sick—no ministry. I drove them forth. She said, "To venture forth is death," and I refused her shelter on her bended knees. And now I know with them I drove Thee forth, refused Thee food and drink and ministry. I sent them to their death and now—O, woe is me!—I also Thee have crucified!

(*She sinks slowly down, shudders, and lies motionless.*)

VOICE.—I will not cast thee off forever.

(*The room grows gradually darker. As the darkness increases, the face of the Crucified becomes brighter and brighter until it glows with dazzling brilliancy. The rays fall on the upturned face of* THE AUNT, *whose features assume a peaceful expression. The eyes of the Crucified lose their reproachful look and reveal nothing but pity. The glow on the face of the Crucified fades imperceptibly as the curtain descends.*)

(*Curtain*)

(*Soft music*)

ACT II

ACT II.

(Time, Christmas Eve. Place, cross-roads in the country. The snow is falling. A man, in the dress of a shepherd, approaches the cross-roads and stops, as if in doubt whether to continue. He examines the guide-post, but fails to make out the inscription.)

SHEPHERD.—It must be near. He said two miles, and I've gone three. The light I seek cannot be far away. A seat beside the fire and somethink from the pot would warm me in and out.

(He examines the guide-post closely, trying to decipher the lettering.)

SHEPHERD.—My old eyes find it hard enough to read by day; they are no good at all by night. I think I'll trudge along a bit, and, if I find I'm wrong, I can put back and take the other road.

(A feeble, wailing sound is heard). What's that? *(Listens.)* It was the wind. What could it be, on such a night as this? Here comes another way-farer, belated like myself. He'll set me on my road.

(A man, in the dress of a drover, approaches. He does not notice THE SHEPHERD until almost upon him.)

SHEPHERD.—Evening, brother.

DROVER *(startled, but quickly recovering from his surprise)*.—Evening.

SHEPHERD.—What seek ye?

DROVER.—A light.

SHEPHERD.—Whither bound?

DROVER.—THE CARTER's stable.

SHEPHERD.—I'd been there now but for the snow.

DROVER.—Why do you tarry here?

SHEPHERD.—I only wait to know which road to take.

DROVER.—Methinks I see a light through yonder trees.

SHEPHERD.—How far think you we have to go?

(*A wailing sound is heard.*)

DROVER (*listening*).—What is't?

SHEPHERD.—The wind.

DROVER.--'Tis somethink else.

SHEPHERD.—What say'st thou?

DROVER.—Somethink alive.

SHEPHERD.—Somethink alive? What, pray?

DROVER.—I'm puzzled, but 'tis alive.

SHEPHERD.—'Tis nothing with split hoofs.

DROVER (*listening attentively to the wailing sound*).—Nor paws.

SHEPHERD (*surprised*).—What think you then?

DROVER (*cautiously*). — There may be things abroad to-night.

SHEPHERD.—Why, man, 'tis Christmas Eve!

DROVER.—Didst think I thought it was All-Hallows?

SHEPHERD.—What meant ye then?

DROVER (*slowly*).—'Tis said the barnyard cattle all have speech this night.

SHEPHERD.—Well?

DROVER.—If such be true, there might be other things.

SHEPHERD (*laying his hand on* THE DROVER's *arm*).—Not so loud. What mean you? Speak.

DROVER (*glancing apprehensively about him and lowering his voice*).—Spirits.

SHEPHERD (*nervously*).—What kind?

DROVER.—The kind that— Look! There comes somethink. (*Draws nearer his companion.*)

SHEPHERD.—'Tis human, man. There's naught to fear.

(*A man dressed as a carter approaches.*)

SHEPHERD.—Evening.

CARTER.—Evening.

DROVER.—Evening.

SHEPHERD (*recognizing the newcomer*).—'Tis THE CARTER.

DROVER.—So it is.

CARTER.—'Tis THE SHEPHERD! How goes it? (*Turning toward* THE DROVER.) And THE DROVER! Whither are ye going?

SHEPHERD.—To seek a place beside your fire and sommat from the pot.

DROVER.—I saw your light and would there, too, same as THE SHEPHERD.

CARTER.—Saw my light? Ye're *daffy*, man!

DROVER.—I saw it there between the trees. I showed it to ye, SHEPHERD; didn't I?

SHEPHERD (*nodding vigorously*).—That's what ye did.

CARTER (*angrily*).—I tell ye no! Ye could not see my light!

DROVER. — 'Twas there (*pointing toward the trees*), between the trees.

CARTER (*more angrily*).—I tell ye no!

SHEPHERD.—He did. He showed it me.

CARTER (*looking at the two men curiously*).—What ails ye? My light's not there. (*Pointing in an entirely opposite direction.*) 'Tis just beyond the hill.

DROVER (*stubbornly*).—I saw the light through the trees.

SHEPHERD (*emphatically*).—And so did I.

CARTER.—There is no dwelling hereabouts but mine, within three miles.

DROVER (*unconvinced*).—I saw the light.

SHEPHERD (*nodding solemnly*).—And so did I.

CARTER (*listening*).—Hark! There it is again! didst hear it?

DROVER.—What?

CARTER.—That cry.

SHEPHERD (*drawing near the two others*).—What is't?

DROVER.—'Tis alive.

CARTER.—I heard it as I sat beside the fire. 'Tis the wind, says I. It came again and louder. 'Tis the wind, says I. At last I left my place beside the fire and opened just a bit the door. 'Tis not the wind, says I. I'll go outside and see. I could na' rest until I knew. I've tramped about to find what 'tis. It is no wind. 'Tis somethink else—

SHEPHERD (*nervously*).—What?

DROVER.—Somethink alive?

CARTER (*slowly*).—Yes, alive.

DROVER.—With neither hoof nor paws.

CARTER.—What are ye saying, DROVER?

DROVER.—'Tis spirits, I believe.

SHEPHERD (*to* CARTER).—I was telling him, as you came up, 'tis Christmas Eve and not All-Hallows.

(*The cry becomes more plaintive. The men listen and look at one another, as though the same thought had occurred to each one at the same moment.*)

SHEPHERD (*nervously*).—What think you, CARTER?

CARTER (*gazing steadily toward the clump of trees, ignoring* THE SHEPHERD's *question*).—See there! between the trees! (*Excitedly.*) Look! what can it be? There's neither hut nor dwelling here save mine!

DROVER.—Perhaps some tramp or gipsy folk's encamped among the trees.

CARTER.—There be none here this season, man. They'd *perish* in the snow!

SHEPHERD (*eagerly*).—What is't then?

CARTER (*thoughtfully*).—Somethink I can't make out.

DROVER.—Spirits.

CARTER.—Alive or dead, I'll soon find out.

SHEPHERD.—Better leave well enough alone. A place beside the fire and sommat from the pot for me. Not so, DROVER?

DROVER.—I think with CARTER, it were well to know what 'tis.

CARTER.—Well said. Come on!

(THE CARTER *starts toward the group of trees, through which a glow is distinctly visible, followed by* THE DROVER.)

SHEPHERD (*anxiously*).—Don't leave me here alone!

CARTER.—Come on, then.

SHEPHERD.—Let's to your roof!

CARTER.—The roof can wait till after.

DROVER.—Let us be off to see what lies behind the trees.

SHEPHERD.—Let's to the fire and sommat from the pot.

CARTER (*impatiently*).—Come, else I go alone.

DROVER (*to* SHEPHERD).—Don't play the woman.

SHEPHERD (*resignedly*).—Go on. I'll follow.

CARTER.—I'll lead the way.

(THE CARTER *and* THE DROVER *walk toward the group* of *trees from which issues the mysterious glow.* THE SHEPHERD *follows reluctantly. They pause in front* of *the clump, as if in doubt whether to venture in. After a brief hesitation,* THE CARTER *starts forward.*)

CARTER.—Come, let's in.

DROVER (*to* SHEPHERD).—Come!

SHEPHERD (*trembling visibly*).—It's worse to stay behind alone than go with them. (*To* DROVER.) Go on! I'll follow.

(THE CARTER *and* THE DROVER *disappear among the trees, but* THE SHEPHERD's *courage fails him at the very last moment, and he remains behind. The wailing has ceased. The stage becomes dark, except the clump* of *trees, which is lighted sufficiently to enable* THE SHEPHERD *to be seen.*)

SHEPHERD (*glancing over his shoulder*).—Mayhap THE DROVER's right. There may be things abroad, on Christmas Eve we know naught of. And yet I thought, on Holy Night, no evil thing could cast its spell on those who make the sign and go to church, whene'er they can (*glancing around*). I wonder where they be and what they've found. I'd go and see, but 'tis better I stay here (*reassuring himself*). I'm not afraid! Why should I be? And yet (*doubtfully*) this glow! I like it not. Once, while the sheep were grazing on the moor, I fell asleep. When I awoke, the gloaming had come on, and it grew dark

afore I got the sheep in fold. As we came home I
saw a willy-wisp. 'Twas somethink like this glow,
and yet 'twas not. I could not leave the sheep, or I'd
have gone to chase the willy-wisp. I know the fish,
the fowl, and furry things that live outside beneath
the sky. I know them all, their seasons, and their
ways. The fields, the wood, the sky are like a book
which I can read as well as the old Vicar does the
big, red-covered ones upon his shelves. I saw them
once—more than a hundred—the time he sent for me
to ask about the lad that perished in the snow upon
the moor. I'm not afraid of all the willy-wisps that
ever was, but somehow I feel queer (*impatiently*).
Why don't they come? I wish that I'd gone, too.
How still it is! The wind is down. I'm glad that
sound's no longer in my ears (*looking about him*).
There's something strange about this place. I never
felt this way before. Not when we found the Farrier
buried in the bog, up to his chin, and three weeks
dead! They left me all alone with him two mortal
hours, but I did not feel as I do now. (*He glances
about him and then looks at the sky.*) The clouds
have disappeared. The stars will soon be out. Why,
there is one I never saw before (*gazing silently at
the star*). Why, yes, of course, I have. It's Holy
Night, and that's the Bethlehem Star—the one the
shepherds saw at night among the hills. A better
name for it would be the Shepherds' Star. They
saw it first and heard the angels singing "Peace on
earth." It was their star. I've heard my mother
tell of the Wise Men. Let's see. How many were
there? Three, I think, she said—who followed close
behind the Bethlehem Star. I learned a Christmas

hymn, when I was but a child. Let's see, how did it go? 'Tis many a year since I have tried to sing it. 'Twas somethink such as this:

(*Shepherds' Song*)
Into the dark Judean skies
The shepherds gazed with awestruck eyes,
And heard the Heavenly chorus sing
The praises of the new-born King.

And by the following of the star
The Wise Men coming from afar
Within the Manger find the Child,
Amid the oxen meek and mild.

They kneel and worship Him as King,
Present the royal gifts they bring,
The gifts for centuries foretold—
Of myrrh, of frankincense and gold.

(*After a brief pause, exultantly.*) There! What would the old mother say to that? 'Tis many a year since I learned it at her knee. She gave me a cake each time I learned a verse, and when I knew it all, a big tart all my own—a gooseberry tart it was—it's all as plain as 'twere but yesterday. 'Tis Christmas Eve, but there've been other Holy Nights than this a-plenty, and I've never sung the hymn. Why then to-night? 'Tis strange. Somethink is in the air, I know not what (*gazing thoughtfully at the star*). I wonder if that's the star the other shepherds saw on Holy Night, nigh on two thousand years ago! The Bethlehem Star did move, they say, until it stood above the stable, Just as this star now stands above my head. How bright it shines! How large! It looks almost as big as a new moon, seen through a pair of sleepy eyes. The Bethlehem Star! The Shepherds' Star! It seems much nearer than the rest.

(*A rabbit issues from the thicket and grazes* THE SHEPHERD's *legs in passing. He gives a start.*)

SHEPHERD.—What's that? (*Peering anxiously after the rabbit.*) Why (*in a tone of relief*), it's only a cony. I wonder what keeps them so long! Let's see. What was I thinking of? Oh, yes, the star.

(*A dark object passes within arm's length.* THE SHEPHERD *jumps back in alarm, and utters a cry of fear.*)

SHEPHERD (*peering anxiously at the object*).— Why, 'tis only a red deer after all. The timid thing would never harm a child. What brings so many creatures out? The wood is all alive!

(*Something whizzes past his head, nearly knocking off his cap. He jumps back with a cry.*)

SHEPHERD (*recovering from his fright*).—'Twas just a grouse roosting among the trees. Perhaps a big-horned owl or something else disturbed it. Once, when I was young, my mother told me of a man—

(*Something runs between* THE SHEPHERD's *legs. He starts so suddenly, he loses his balance, trips and falls into the snow. He picks himself up with difficulty, and sees a fox sitting on his haunches nearby and watching the glow shining through the trees.*)

SHEPHERD.—He gave me a start, he did, that fox!

(*A whirring sound is heard.* THE SHEPHERD *listens. A golden pheasant alights close by.*)

SHEPHERD (*suddenly*).—Hark! I hear somethink moving among the trees. They're coming! Now, I'll know what kept them both so long.

(THE CARTER *appears, carrying the body of a woman in his arms.* THE WOMAN *is thinly clad and has no outer garment. Her head rests on* THE CARTER'S *shoulder, her eyes are closed, giving the appearance of a person either asleep or unconscious.*

THE DROVER *next appears, carrying a small burden, wrapped in a woman's cloak. He holds it awkwardly, as though afraid of dropping it.*

The glow follows them to the center, leaving the rest of the stage in partial darkness. The star changes its position, and stands directly above them.

THE SHEPHERD *gazes at the men in speechless amazement. The various animals form a semicircle in the snow as near to the men as possible, and then remain motionless during the dialogue which follows.*)

SHEPHERD (*dazed*).—What have ye there? What kept ye?

CARTER.—We found her in the snow—and waited.

SHEPHERD.—For what?

CARTER (*pointing to the bundle in* THE DROVER'S *arms*).—That.

SHEPHERD.—That?

CARTER.—Don't ye understand?

SHEPHERD (*bewildered*).—No.

DROVER.—Ye hear*d* it crying, man.

SHEPHERD.—You don't mean—

DROVER (*nodding*).—Yes.

SHEPHERD.—Is it a boy?

DROVER.—Yes.

SHEPHERD.—'Tis many a lam*b* I've found amid the snow, but (*turning to* THE CARTER) how fare*s* the mother? Is she safe?

CARTER.—She'*s* nearly in, *poor* thing. 'Twas terrible!

DROVER.—'Twa*s* so indee*d*, and all alone.

SHEPHERD.—Alone? The light? Who *b*uilt the fire?

CARTER.—There was no fire.

SHEPHERD.—We saw the light a-shining through the tree*s*.

DROVER.—There was no fire, I tell ye, man.

SHEPHERD (*puzzled*).—No fire? Whence came the light?

CARTER.—I tell ye there was none.

DROVER.—No, nothink.

SHEPHERD (*angrily*).—Think ye to *p*lay the fool with me? I saw it.

CARTER.—Come now, enough of thi*s*! We mus*t* be off.

SHEPHERD.—Whither are ye bound? The hour grow*s* late.

CARTER.—To *s*eek the *s*helter of my roof.

SHEPHERD.—Is't far?

CARTER.—Hard by. 'Tis but a *rough* place, but she's welcome to it. Come!

SHEPHERD (*approaching* THE CARTER *and making a motion to relieve him of his burden*).—Give her to me and rest awhile.

CARTER.—No, follow me.

SHEPHERD (*to* DROVER).—Give me the child.

DROVER.—I'll *carry* it myself.

CARTER.—Make haste. She's like to die. Her clothes are frozen stiff. Let's go!

SHEPHERD.—I've naught to do but follow. 'Tis many a lamb I've carried in my breast.

(THE CARTER *with his burden leads the way,* THE DROVER *follows with* THE CHILD, THE SHEPHERD *last of all.*

The glow accompanies them and the star moves with them directly above their heads.

The deer crosses the stage and follows the procession. Rabbits, hares, pheasants, grouse and smaller birds issue from among the trees and follow the deer until they disappear among the trees. The fox brings up the rear.

A band of Waits enters from the opposite side, singing, and halts in the center of the stage. The star has disappeared, but a soft light suffuses the scene.)

"O, All Ye Beasts and Cattle."

The mild and patient oxen
  Stand awestruck at the sight,
The manger rude that holds their food
  Holds something else to-night.
A little babe amid the kine,
  Upon its mother's arm,
Around its head and lowly bed
  A light shines pure and calm.

The mild and patient oxen
  Stand spell-bound by the sound,
For voices clear each list'ning ear
  With melody surround;
The little babe amid the kine
  Smiles on its mother's breast;
Above its head with wings outspread
  The heavenly chorus rest.

The mild and patient oxen
  The Wise Men now behold;
As for a king rich gifts they bring,
  Myrrh, frankincense and gold;
The little babe amid the kine
  They worship and adore,
While o'er its head with wings outspread
  The holy angels soar.

The mild and patient oxen
  Kneel down amid the straw
About the bed, within the shed,
  In wonder mixed with awe;
The little babe amid the kine
  They hear acclaimed a King,
And from afar they see the star
  And hear the angels sing.

Come let us, too, adore Him
On this most holy night;
The star will guide us to His side
If we but seek its light;
The little babe amid the kine
We, too, may hail as King,
Like men of old, our myrrh and gold
And frankincense may bring.

(*While the Waits are singing the last stanza the rear of the stage opens and discloses the interior of the Stable at Bethlehem. Mary and Joseph are seen with the Child in their midst. The Wise Men are kneeling in front of the Manger, while oxen and sheep are grouped about them.*

Celestial Voices are heard singing "Adeste Fideles."

The Waits kneel in the snow.)

(*Tableau.*)

(*Curtain*)

ACT III

ACT III.

(*The interior* of THE CARTER's *home, a combination* of *stable and dwelling. A fire is burning in a rude stone fire-place in the back. On either side* of *the fire-place are shelves containing dishes, pots and pans. From the rafters hang pieces* of *harness, rope and chains; near the fire are sides* of *bacon, strings* of *onions, herbs, and woolen sacks, containing meal and flour. In the corner farthest from the fire is a pile* of *hay. On the side opposite is a manger, about six feet long and three feet wide, one end* of *which abuts against the wall, the other extends into the room, affording space on each side for two animals to feed at the same time. The manger is filled with hay. A donkey and a goat are standing, eating hay from the manger as the curtain goes up.*

The door opens and THE CARTER *enters, carrying* THE WOMAN. *He is followed by* THE DROVER *with* THE CHILD. THE SHEPHERD *enters last.*)

CARTER (*going straight to the manger and depositing* THE WOMAN *on the hay inside, thrusting aside the two animals*).

DROVER.—What shall I do with it?

CARTER.—Sit down by the fire!

(THE DROVER *seats himself beside the fire with* THE CHILD *in his arms and uncovers its face.*)

CARTER.—I'll light a tallow dip.

SHEPHERD (*in amazement*).—Look!

49

(*He points to* THE DROVER *and* THE CHILD. THE CARTER *turns and glances in the same direction. Both men stand petrified. A glow comes from the group by the fire sufficiently bright to light the interior, making the additional light unnecessary.*)

CARTER (*recovering from his astonishment*).—'Tis nothink to hurt us. DROVER's not afraid. Let's have a look!

(*He approaches* THE CHILD, *followed by* THE SHEPHERD. *They gaze in silence on the infant's countenance. While they are gazing, the donkey and the goat approach the group and stand motionless.*)

DROVER.—Didst ever see so fine a child?

CARTER.—I'm no judge, but I'm of your opinion.

SHEPHERD.—The same with me.

CARTER (*going to the pot beside the fire and lifting the lid*).—THE WOMAN yonder must have sommat hot. Take off her shoes and wrap her feet in my old blanket while I stir the broth.

(*He busies himself preparing the broth. Meanwhile* THE SHEPHERD *hastens to carry out* THE CARTER's *instructions.*)

SHEPHERD.—Her feet be like two lumps of ice.

CARTER (*bending over his cooking*).—Rub them, but have a care!

(THE SHEPHERD *takes* THE WOMAN's *feet in his hands and endeavors to restore the circulation by a gentle friction. When he has finished he wraps them in a blanket.*)

50

CARTER (*approaching the manger, cup in hand*). —Raise her head and hold it while I feed her with the spoon. Not so roughly, man! Women are not sheep. There now, steady!

(THE CARTER *succeeds, after several failures, in forcing some of the hot broth down* THE WOMAN'S *throat. The two men wait anxiously to see the effect.*)

SHEPHERD.—She's not so white. There's color in her cheeks.

CARTER.—Hush! She's coming to. I'll fix a pillow for her head.

(*He takes a small sack hanging from the rafters, thrusts hay inside, and brings it to the manger.*)

CARTER.—There! rest her head on this. That's better. Fetch me that smock hanging on yonder peg, to wrap around her shoulders. (THE SHEPHERD *fetches the smock.*) There, now! We'll bide a bit and then more broth.

(*They leave* THE WOMAN *and return to the fire.* THE CARTER *takes three bowls and spoons from the shelf, places them on the hearth, fills them from the pot, and motions to the others.*)

CARTER.—Draw up and eat.

SHEPHERD.—Give me THE CHILD. I'll hold him while you eat.

DROVER.—I've neither hunger nor thirst.

SHEPHERD.—Give me THE CHILD and rest your arms.

DROVER.—There is no weight upon them.

SHEPHERD.—'Tis many a lamb I've carried in my breast. Give it to me.

CARTER.—Your broth is cooling.

SHEPHERD.—I'd rather hold THE CHILD.

CARTER.—Eat first.

(THE SHEPHERD takes his bowl and empties it in silence.)

WOMAN (*feebly*).—Water.

CARTER (*approaching the manger with a cup*).— Drink!

WOMAN (*draining the cup*).—Thank you.

CARTER.—Now try to sleep.

(*She closes her eyes.* THE CARTER *watches her for a few minutes and then goes back to join the others near the fire.*)

SHEPHERD (*laying the empty bowl on the hearth*). —Give me the child and eat.

DROVER.—I want nothink.

SHEPHERD.—Ye said ye'd hunger a while back.

DROVER.—I had.

SHEPHERD.—And now?

DROVER.—'Tis gone.

(*A sound is heard outside. A door between the manger and the fold opens and a young man enters, followed by a draft-horse wearing a heavy harness. The young man advances a few steps, then stops suddenly and stands gazing at the group near the fire. The horse, instead of going directly to the manger, stands motionless within the frame of the door. A hare and a rabbit enter and run straight toward the spot where the donkey and goat are standing. They sit upon their haunches and appear to have lost all fear of men. A moment later a fox issues from beneath the body of the cart-horse and joins the other animals. The hare and rabbit do not notice him, and the fox does not appear to be conscious of their presence.*

The silence is finally broken by a knock on the outer door. THE CARTER goes to the door and opens it. A man with a peddler's pack stands on the door-stone.)

CARTER.—Well?

PEDDLER.—Shelter. I have wherewith to pay.

CARTER.—Enter! I turn no one this night away. 'Tis Christmas Eve.

(*THE PEDDLER enters and makes directly for the fire. Halfway across the room he hesitates and comes to a standstill.*

A pheasant and a grouse come in through the open door and join the animals by the fire before the door closes.)

CARTER.—Draw near the fire. There's still something in the pot. Hast supped?

PEDDLER.—I've nothink since the morn, and yet the hunger, keen enough a short bit back, is gone.

CARTER.—Gone!

PEDDLER.—Since I stepped 'cross your threshold, 'tis as though I'd never known the *pangs*.

SHEPHERD (*to* PEDDLER).—Come nearer. 'Tis a bonny CHILD. As fine a boy as ever was. Come look!

PEDDLER.—A *child*? I'll have a look.

(*He approaches* THE CHILD *in* THE DROVER'S *arms and bends over the infant.*)

SHEPHERD.—Didst ever see so fine a boy?

PEDDLER (*gazing silently, and then turning slowly to* THE CARTER).—Whence came THE CHILD?

SHEPHERD (*interrupting*).—Didst ever see its like?

CARTER.—Born in the snow, this night.

PEDDLER.—The mother?

CARTER (*pointing toward the manger*).—There.

PEDDLER (*turning and observing the sleeping* WOMAN *for the first time*).—She sleeps. 'Tis well.

SHEPHERD.—'Tis many a ewe I've seen die in the snow.

PEDDLER.—Poor creatures!

SHEPHERD.—The lambs I've carried in my bosom to the kitchen fire, only to find them *dead*.

PEDDLER.—'Tis a miracle they lived.

SHEPHERD (*misunderstanding*).—They died more often than they lived.

CARTER.—But not this night.

DROVER.—Five minutes more, and 'twere too late.

SHEPHERD.—We've done a good night's work.

YOUNG MAN.—If the old mare had not gone lame I'd given ye all a lift

SHEPHERD (to DROVER).—Give me THE CHILD!

DROVER.—Hush! 'Tis fast asleep.

CARTER (to PEDDLER).—How comes it I have never seen you here before?

PEDDLER.—Our paths have never crossed until tonight.

CARTER.—I know the people hereabouts for thirty mile or more. None pass my door without a stop to rest themselves and chat.

SHEPHERD.—What have you in your pack?

PEDDLER (to CARTER).—Didst say you found them in the snow?

CARTER.—Seated beside the fire, I heard the infant's wail, and ventured forth. I could not rest, and sought until I found them there, among the trees.

PEDDLER.—How?

CARTER.—The glow. The same as is here now. We saw the light and followed it.

PEDDLER.—As did the three Wise Men.

CARTER.—THE CHILD was wrapped inside her cloak.

SHEPHERD.—The lamb born in the snow.

(THE PEDDLER, stepping back far enough to allow his glance to include THE WOMAN and the group *about* THE CHILD, *lets his pack slip from his shoulder to the ground.*)

PEDDLER (*slowly*).—Born in the snow, on Christmas Eve! (*Resuming, after a brief interval.*) Full many a year I've tramped it with my pack, beneath the summer suns and winter stars. Strange are the sights I've seen and stranger yet the men I've met! There's many a tale between the covers of a book, not half so weird and fear-compelling as the living ones of which I was a part. I've tramped it in strange lands and crossed wide seas. I've bargained with strange people in strange tongues, and everywhere I've found that men, however much they differ in their dress and speech, at heart are brothers. And red blood flows within the veins of all. Their loves and passions are the same. Gold, honor, fame are everywhere the ends for which men strive. While now and then, some great soul lifts its voice and points its finger toward the higher, upward way. Such souls are rare. They come and go and leave a trail of light behind to mark their progress. Not like the conquerors of the world, whose path to glory was outlined by smoking roofs and bleeding forms, by ghostly trails of whitening bones, by ruined cities, and by woman's moans, but by the power of an idea these souls have wrought. They came not to enslave, but to set free, and gave their all—yes, life itself— to help advance their cause. I've seen such men in other lands, and known them for my brothers. Yes, brothers of the Man who came to earth, a little child on Christmas Eve, two thousand years ago. I thought of Him to-night as I was tramping through

56

the snow. I raised my eyes, and lo! I saw the star above my head—the Bethlehem Star—and, as I walked, it went before, until at last I came unto this place. With senses all alert I heard sounds until now unheard, and saw sights hitherto unseen. As I approached this roof, the trees were all alive with birds. Across my path ran hares and tiny rabbits, oftentimes so close they brushed my garments, and seemed to know no fear. I passed a noble buck with spreading horns, beside his mate, and neither moved. They stood outside, a few feet from the door; and as I passed did not vouchsafe a look at me. Upon the eaves, above the door, a snow-white owl was perched, and everywhere were tracks of tiny, furry things, all leading to the door. It was as though some magnet drew them hence; and there they sat, some on their haunches, others on all fours, facing the door and listening, as it were. I paused and waited ere I knocked, and wondered why so many enemies were crouched like friends, instead of tearing at each other's throats. I've wandered far in many lands, but never have I seen the like before.

WOMAN.—CARTER.

CARTER (*approaching the manger*).—What is't?

WOMAN.—THE CHILD?

CARTER.—'Tis well. It sleeps.

WOMAN.—THE CHILD?

CARTER (*going to the fire and returning with a cup of broth*).—Here, drink. Then sleep.

WOMAN (*refusing the cup*).—No, no, THE CHILD.

CARTER (*offering the cup again*).—Drink first!

(THE WOMAN *swallows a little of the broth unwillingly, then pushes the cup away.*)

WOMAN.—THE CHILD.

CARTER (*in a tone of authority*).—Let her have it!

(THE CARTER *takes* THE CHILD *from* THE DROVER *and places it in* THE WOMAN'S *arms. The manger is suffused by a glow emanating from* THE WOMAN *and* THE CHILD. *The corners of the room are dark.* THE CARTER, THE SHEPHERD *and* THE DROVER *stand side by side facing the manger.* THE YOUNG MAN *advances, followed by the horse, and takes a like position behind the manger.* THE PEDDLER *gathers up his pack and stands with his back toward the door, facing the manger and the three men. The donkey and the goat, with the fox, hare and rabbit, group themselves along the manger opposite the feet of* THE WOMAN. *The pheasant and grouse perch on the edge of the manger.* THE WOMAN *uncovers* THE CHILD'S *face and gazes in silent rapture upon its features. After a brief interval she opens the cloak in which* THE CHILD *is wrapped. The glow becomes instantly more intense and increases until the faces of the mother,* THE CHILD, *the men and the animals' forms are distinctly visible. The remainder of the interior is in the shadow.*

THE PEDDLER *opens his pack and takes out a fine gold chain. He aproaches the manger and lays it in* THE CHILD'S *hands.* THE WOMAN *lifts her eyes to* THE PEDDLER'S *face and smiles gratefully.*

58

THE CARTER *goes to the shelf beside the fire-place,* *opens a box, takes out a candle made of bees' wax, and returning to the manger, places it beside* THE CHILD. THE WOMAN *gives him a smile of thanks.*

THE DROVER *draws a large, greasy leathern wallet from his inner breast-pocket, opens it, and carefully removes a small package wrapped in white paper, containing a few grains of musk, taken from the wild musk ox. He lays the package beside the candle. The mother smiles her thanks.*

THE SHEPHERD *draws a moss-agate stone from his pocket. The stone has a smooth polish and has evidently been treasured carefully for years. One side is beautifully mottled; on the other in the center are lines forming a perfect cross.* THE SHEPHERD *approaches the manger and starts to place the stone beside the candle and the packet, but drops it. The stone falls upon* THE CHILD's *breast, on which its tiny arms are folded. As soon as it touches* THE CHILD's *body, one of the small hands opens, grasps the stone, and closes tightly.* THE WOMAN *turns pale, gives* THE SHEPHERD *a frightened look, and closes her eyes, while a tear rolls down each cheek.* THE CHILD *looks up into* THE SHEPHERD's *face and smiles.* THE WOMAN *tightens her hold upon* THE CHILD *as if to ward off an impending danger.*

THE YOUNG MAN *behind the manger takes a ruddy-cheeked apple from his pocket and lays it beside the other offerings.*

The pheasant spreads his wings. His largest, most brilliantly colored feather floats slowly downward and lies across THE WOMAN's *limbs.)*

PEDDLER.—Who gives the thing he holds most dear receives more than he gives. We toil and save —for what? To spend upon ourselves. We hoard our treasures. Why? To lose them, soon or late. 'Tis only when we give with generous hand and willing heart that we retain our own. For thieves break through and steal the things we hoard and hide. Time crumbles and corrodes the shining things that please the eye. We give our youth, our manhood, even age, to gain the glittering spoils, torn from the breast of Mother Earth. For what? When Death comes knocking at our door and bids us open, what avails the treasure we have sweat and toiled for through the years. Naked and empty-handed as we came, we go from earth. It matters little then how full or empty all our coffers are. Can gold and lands and earthly honors for one instant stay the hand that knocks on each man's door, purchase a moment's respite, grant reprieve? Too late, alas! too late!

(THE PEDDLER *pauses and his head sinks sadly on his breast. After a brief interval of silence he resumes.*)

PEDDLER.—Too late for those who only stood with hands outstretched to take, whose livelong cry of "More!" was ever on their lips.

WOMAN (*lifting her head slightly*).—But what of those who gave? Not gold alone, but, better still, their strength, their lives, their love?.

PEDDLER.—All that they gave, they had—and more.

(*THE WOMAN'S head falls back. She breathes a sigh of content.*)

CARTER.—THE CHILD is welcome to the candle.

DROVER.—And to the scent.

YOUNG MAN.—And to the apple.

SHEPHERD.—And to the little stone.

(*The door opens slowly to admit a bird and then closes. The bird flies into the room, circles above the heads of the people for a moment, and then perches on the edge of the manger near THE WOMAN's head. From there it hops to her wrist, and drops something from its beak into her hand. THE WOMAN looks at the object doubtfully and then suddenly recognizes it. Her face flushes and a smile radiates her countenance.*)

WOMAN.—My ring!

(*She toys with it lovingly, and then slips it on the fourth finger of her left hand. The bird meanwhile perches on the edge of the manger near THE WOMAN's head. THE WOMAN turns and gives it a loving glance.*)

WOMAN.—Dear little bird!

(*The bird bursts into a flood of melody. THE CHILD looks up at the bird and smiles.*)

PEDDLER (*listening, then turning toward the door*).—There's something trying to get in!

(*He opens the door. A huge dog bounds into the room, carrying a paper in his mouth. He goes straight to the manger and drops the paper in THE*

WOMAN's *lap. She glances at the paper, then utters a cry of joy.*)

WOMAN.—My marriage lines! I lost them in the snow. (*Laying her hand on the dog's head.*) Dear, noble beast!

(*She allows her hand to rest motionless on the dog's head. The animal evinces his delight by wagging his tail violently and uttering a half a dozen deep-toned barks. THE CHILD looks up at the dog and smiles. As soon as the latter perceives this, he ceases barking and draws as close to the manger as possible, whimpering beside himself with delight.*)

PEDDLER.—Man, bird and beast hath given of his best unto this CHILD, born in the snow on Christmas Eve, and to the mother that which, next her CHILD, is dearer far than all—her ring and marriage lines, the seal and patent of maternity. Despite man's cruelty and selfishness, which drove her forth to die alone at night amid the storm, she shall live on for ages, wearing woman's crown with sweet humility. Forgotten now the bitter anguish and the pain; nothing remains but joy because her CHILD is born.

(THE WOMAN *clasps her* CHILD *more closely in her arms and gazes at its face with rapture.*)

PEDDLER (*continuing*).—This CHILD shall also live, and with its tiny hands bind all mankind into one brotherhood. Its smile shall banish grief and lighten weary hearts. Its fingers shall point out the path that leads to life beyond this earthly vale of tears. The road its tiny feet shall travel shall be forever free from pitfalls and from harm. The light about its head a beacon on the endless shores of Time to guide the weary traveler on his way.

(*During the apostrophe to* THE CHILD, *the glow becomes brighter and brighter, until of dazzling whiteness.* THE CARTER, THE DROVER, THE SHEPHERD *fall upon their knees.* THE YOUNG MAN *emerges from behind the manger and kneels back of the other men. The animals and birds retain their previous positions as if carved from stone.* THE PEDDLER *alone remains standing with arms outstretched.*)

PEDDLER (*slowly, with great solemnity*).—A little CHILD shall lead them. So long as this endures, the world shall live. Against its tiny form the waves of doubt, of sin, of death, shall beat in vain.

WOMAN (*straining* THE CHILD *to her breast*).— My CHILD, my little CHILD!

PEDDLER.—Within its tiny hands the world's hope rests, a hope that never dies, yet born anew each Christmas Eve, revives within men's hearts the spark of faith, which keeps their feet from stumbling in the midnight darkness of the soul. Man's strength is feeble at the most. The way is long and dark, with perils manifold. Hope is the light that shines upon the way, and in this CHILD I see the promise of the life to be.

WOMAN.—My CHILD, my little CHILD.

PEDDLER (*very slowly*).—Its tiny hands must yet be pierced by nails. Its little brow must grow to fit the thorns. Its tender feet must bleed to mark the way. Its feeble shoulder bared to scourging rods.

63

WOMAN.—O, say not so! It cannot, must not be!

PEDDLER (*sadly*).—It can and must!

WOMAN.—Is there no other way?

PEDDLER.—None.

WOMAN.—But he is innocent.

PEDDLER.—It matters not.

WOMAN.—Too innocent to suffer so.

PEDDLER.—By suffering alone he may attain

WOMAN.—He is my CHILD—

PEDDLER.—His Father's also.

WOMAN.—His father's dead.

PEDDLER.—His Father lives.

WOMAN.—He's all I have.

PEDDLER.—It is the only way.

WOMAN.—The only way?

PEDDLER.—To keep your CHILD.

WOMAN (*dreamily*).—His tiny hands pierced by the nails! (*Pausing.*) His little forehead crowned with thorns! (*Pausing.*) His little, tender feet all bruised and bleeding! (*Pausing.*) His dimpled shoulders scourged with rods! (*Shuddering.*) I cannot, O! I cannot!

PEDDLER.—Alas! poor mother!

WOMAN.—I'll flee at dawn and hide him safe from all who wish him harm.

PEDDLER.—There is no hiding-place. 'Twere vain to try.

WOMAN.—Take me and let him go!

PEDDLER.—It cannot be.

WOMAN.—Take me, take me, but let him go!

PEDDLER.—The cup is for his lips alone.

WOMAN.—Give it to me. I'll drain it to the dregs.

PEDDLER.—'Tis not for you.

WOMAN (*firmly*).—He's my CHILD.

PEDDLER.—To give, but not to keep.

WOMAN.—What if I should refuse?

PEDDLER.—You would not dare—

WOMAN (*interrrupting*).—A mother dares all for her CHILD—

PEDDLER.—Destroy the whole world's hope.

(THE WOMAN *trembles violently and raises* THE CHILD's *hand containing the stone to her lips.*)

WOMAN (*humbly*).—I kiss the cross submissive to my fate.

PEDDLER (*extending his arms and gazing toward the ceiling above the manger*).—And for this sacrifice I see thee sitting, crowned, amidst the heavenly hosts, the Queen of Heaven, blessed above, beyond all womankind. Thou gav'st the world the thing to thee most dear, and what thou gavest thou hast still, and mortals through thy gift, this Holy Night, shall do thee homage for all time.

(*The roof above the manger opens. Three angels are seen hovering above* THE WOMAN *and* THE

CPSIA information can be obtained
at www.ICGtesting.com
Printed in the USA
BVHW04*1049170918
527708BV00015B/2021/P